I0415883

Monitoring Kittlitz's and Marbled Murrelets in Glacier Bay National Park and Preserve

2010 Annual Report

Natural Resource Technical Report NPS/SEAN/NRTR—2011/441

Steven T. Hoekman
Institute of Arctic Biology
University of Alaska
Fairbanks, AK, 99775

Brendan J. Moynahan
Southeast Alaska Network, Inventory and Monitoring Program
National Park Service
3100 National Park Road
Juneau, AK, 99801

Mark S. Lindberg
Institute of Arctic Biology
University of Alaska
Fairbanks, AK, 99775

March 2011

U.S. Department of the Interior
National Park Service
Natural Resource Program Center
Fort Collins, Colorado

The National Park Service, Natural Resource Program Center publishes a range of reports that address natural resource topics of interest and applicability to a broad audience in the National Park Service and others in natural resource management, including scientists, conservation and environmental constituencies, and the public.

The Natural Resource Technical Report Series is used to disseminate results of scientific studies in the physical, biological, and social sciences for both the advancement of science and the achievement of the National Park Service mission. The series provides contributors with a forum for displaying comprehensive data that are often deleted from journals because of page limitations.

All manuscripts in the series receive the appropriate level of peer review to ensure that the information is scientifically credible, technically accurate, appropriately written for the intended audience, and designed and published in a professional manner.

This report received formal peer review by subject-matter experts who were not directly involved in the collection, analysis, or reporting of the data, and whose background and expertise put them on par technically and scientifically with the authors of the information.

Views, statements, findings, conclusions, recommendations, and data in this report do not necessarily reflect views and policies of the National Park Service, U.S. Department of the Interior. Mention of trade names or commercial products does not constitute endorsement or recommendation for use by the U.S. Government.

This report is available the Southeast Alaska Network (http://science.nature.nps.gov/im/units/sean/Default.aspx) and the Natural Resource Publications Management website (http://www.nature.nps.gov/publications/NRPM).

Please cite this publication as:

NPS 132/107036, March 2011

Contents

Figures

Tables

Appendix

Executive Summary

The Southeast Alaska Network (SEAN) has targeted Kittlitz's murrelets (*Brachyramphus brevirostris*) in Glacier Bay National Park and Preserve for long-term monitoring based on concerns arising from evidence of global and local populations declines in this rare seabird. Prior research identified several obstacles to effective monitoring inherent to our study system. In 2009, we implemented boat-based line transect surveys in Glacier Bay proper (hereafter "Glacier Bay") to address these challenges, with an emphasis on testing efficacy of novel survey and analytic methods. Based on these results, we retained use of line transect methods, shore-to-shore transect orientation, spatially-balanced sampling, and analytic methods accounting for incomplete detection and species identification. We further refined methods for 2010 by preferring 2 over 1 survey observers, allocating sampling effort via unequal probability sampling, introducing a local variance estimator for encounter rates, implementing zigzag rather than linear transects in enclosed waters, and increasing sampling coverage of Glacier Bay to include selected non-motorized and critical habitat areas. Our objectives for this report were to 1) describe changes in methods, 2) estimate abundance of Kittlitz's murrelets, and secondarily of marbled murrelets (*B. marmoratus*), in Glacier Bay during July 2010, and 3) place our 2009 and 2010 abundance estimates in meaningful context relative to other recent estimates for Glacier Bay.

We estimated an abundance of $14,503 \pm 1,479$ ($x \pm$ SE) Kittlitz's and $67,259 \pm 5,854$ marbled murrelets in Glacier Bay during July 2010. Abundance of Kittlitz's murrelets in 2010 was similar to 2009, but more than doubled for marbled Murrelets. We found the largest concentrations of both species in open waters in the mid- to lower portions of the main Bay, a distribution that was atypical for Kittlitz's murrelets, which are frequently associated with glacially-influenced habitats in the upper fjords of Glacier Bay. We hypothesized that both species took advantage of exceptionally good foraging opportunities in the main Bay and that the large increase in the 2010 population of marbled murrelets involved immigration from outside Glacier Bay. Abundance estimates for both species from 2009 and 2010 were similar to estimates from concurrent surveys but substantially higher than from previous recent estimates from Glacier Bay. However, these earlier estimates employed strip transect survey methods, which likely were subject to unknown but large and variable negative bias. After adjusting these estimates using reported species identification rates and reasonable assumptions about detection, we concluded it was likely that estimates from strip transects have substantially under-estimated abundance for both species and that populations of marbled murrelets have increased in 2009-2010 relative to 1999-2007. Whether increases in estimated abundance for Kittlitz's in 2009-2010 reflect modest population increase, sampling error, and/or differences in methods remains less clear. We stress that effects of differences in methods on abundance estimates cannot be fully resolved.

Acknowledgments

We are indebted to our boat captain J. Smith. W. F. Johnson provided indispensable assistance with field operations and data management. We thank S. M. Gende and G. V. Hilderbrand for comments on versions of this report and M. J. Conroy, J. L. Laake, and P. M. Lukcas for comments on our methods. H. Coletti, B. Eichenlaub, S. M. Gende, J. I. Hodges, M. D. Kirchhoff, M. L. Kissling, C. Smith, and W. L. Thompson contributed advice and/or logistic support.

Introduction

The Vital Signs program being implemented by the Southeast Alaska Network (SEAN) seeks to monitor the long-term status and trends of Kittlitz's murrelets in Glacier Bay National Park and Preserve (Moynahan et al. 2008). Selection of this species for long-term monitoring as one of twelve core vital signs by SEAN arose from concern about declines of global and Glacier Bay populations, from its status as a candidate species for protection under the U. S. Endangered Species Act (USFWS 2010) and belief that populations directly relate to drivers of change in this ecosystem (i.e., glacial dynamics, climate change, human activity). In 2009, SEAN embarked on a two-year effort of evaluating alternative sampling and analytic strategies for monitoring. Previous studies in Glacier Bay (Agler et al. 1998, Lindell 2005, Piatt et al. 2007, Drew et al. 2008, Kirchhoff 2008) suggested declines in populations of Kittlitz's murrelets but uncertainty remains, in part because of differences in methods among studies. This research also highlighted several challenges to effective monitoring inherent to the study system: difficulty distinguishing between coexisting Kittlitz's and marbled murrelets, incomplete detection of murrelets, large spatial and temporal variation in populations, and sampling problems arising from convoluted topography. In 2009, a pilot field season built on prior research by testing line transect survey methods and better tailoring field and analytic methods to meet above challenges.

Results from these efforts identified several successful components introduced in 2009 but also suggested further refinements for 2010 surveys (Hoekman et al. 2011a). We implemented distance sampling methods in 2009 and concluded these were superior to commonly used strip transects, which produce negatively biased estimates because of incomplete detection of murrelets within typical 300 m strip widths. Our analyses revealed a slight violation of the critical assumption of line transects of complete detection near the transect center line, but we used analytic methods to account for this discrepancy. An experiment also indicated use of 2 relative to 1 survey observers provided increased efficiency and better adherence to assumptions of methods. Large variation in rates of species identification for coexisting Kittlitz's and marbled murrelets in previous surveys has introduced substantial but variable negative bias to species-specific abundance estimates, but we extended analytic methods for line transects to account for unidentified murrelets (Hoekman et al. 2011b). To mitigate decreased precision of abundance estimates associated with large spatial variation in density, we implemented a Generalized Random Tesselation Stratified (GRTS) sampling design to achieve a spatially-balanced sample (Stevens and Olsen 2004). However, effectiveness our strategy of geographic stratification was reduced by unpredictable aggregations of Kittlitz's murrelets. Therefore, in 2010 we allocated sampling effort relative to expected densities of Kittlitz's murrelets using unequal probability sampling, a tool better suited to patchy populations. We also introduced a local variance estimator that uses spatial correlation to increase precision without requiring *a priori* delineation of strata (Stevens and Olsen 2003). In 2009, we used linear transects oriented perpendicular to the shoreline. This approach provided reasonably representative sampling coverage within convoluted fords, avoided placing transects parallel to observed density gradients of murrelets, and facilitated precise replication of surveys (Kirchhoff *In Review*). However, in very enclosed waters, resulting short transects decreased precision of abundance estimates by increasing travel relative to sampling time and increasing variability in encounter rates among transects. In 2010, zigzag transects in enclosed waters provided benefits of linear transects but also avoided undesirably short transects. We also expanded our sampling area in 2010 to include several non-motorized and critical habitat areas to provide more representative coverage of Glacier Bay.

Our monitoring design and survey methods were driven by our predominant interest in Kittlitz's murrelets. However, because of the importance of distinguishing between coexisting Kittlitz's and marbled murrelets, we present results for both species.

Our objectives for 2010 were to implement refined survey and analytic methods based on findings from 2009 surveys. Here we describe improvements to line transect survey methods, estimate density and abundance of Kittlitz's murrelets (and secondarily of marbled murrelets) in Glacier Bay during July. Because differences in methods have had large influence on abundance estimates, we also strive to place out 2009 and 2010 estimates in meaningful context relative to other recent estimates for Glacier Bay. Specifically, we adjusted abundance estimates to control for differences in methods in order to assess whether recent increases in abundance estimates could plausibly be explained differences in methods. For additional detail on survey methods and results, see the SEAN Kittlitz's Murrelet Monitoring Protocol (Hoekman et al. *In Preparation*).

Methods
Study area and species
Glacier Bay is a narrow, glacial fjord located in Southeast Alaska. In 2010, we augmented our 2009 study area (Hoekman et al. 2011a) with areas within non-motorized and critical habitat. The 2010 study area encompassed 1170 km^2 of waters north of Icy Strait and excluded areas too small to allow safe and easy passage and some non-motorized areas (Fig. 1). The Kittlitz's murrelet is a small, rare seabird endemic to Alaska and northeastern Russia that is closely associated with glacially-influenced habitats and has a significant breeding population in Glacier Bay (Day et al. 1999, Kuletz et al. 2003, USFWS 2010). The Kittlitz's murrelet and the similar but more numerous marbled murrelet coexist in Glacier Bay but cannot always be distinguished (Hoekman et al. 2011a, b). Both species may evade detection by swimming, diving, or flying (Agness et al. 2008, Lukacs et al. 2010, Hoekman et al. 2011a).

Sampling design
As in 2009, we employed a GRTS sampling design (Stevens and Olsen 2004), which allowed us to diminish deleterious effects of large spatial variation in murrelet abundance (Kissling et al. 2007, Drew et al. 2008, Kirchhoff 2008, Hoekman et al. 2011a) by providing a random, yet spatially-balanced sample. In contrast to the geographic stratification implemented in 2009, we allocated survey effort relative to expected densities of Kittlitz's murrelets using unequal probability sampling. Our approach was to group Glacier Bay into 5 regions with similar past densities (Drew et al. 2008) and to adjust inclusion probability for each region so that a doubling of expected density provided a 50% increase in inclusion probability. For a sixth region comprised of areas of special ecological or management significance, we included all transects not selected during probabilistic sample selection. Thus, the probability of inclusion for these added transects was 1. To maximize sample size but avoid problems arising from short transects, we targeted transect lengths of 4-8 km (Drew et al. 2008, Hoekman et al. 2011a). Similar to 2009, we used linear transects in waters >2.5 km wide, with transects traversing the widest portion of Glacier Bay split into 2 (Fig. 1). However, in more enclosed waters we introduced zigzag transects to avoid undesirably short transects (Fig. 2). To avoid placing transects parallel to the observed density gradient of murrelets relative to water depth (Drew et al. 2008, Kirchhoff 2008, Kirchhoff *In Review*) and to provide representative coverage across water depths, we oriented linear transects perpendicular to the local prevailing shoreline and zigzag transects from shore-to-shore.

Field methods
We conducted boat-based line transect surveys (Buckland et al. 2001) aboard the U. S. National Park Service R/V Capelin using methods similar to 2009. Observers classified murrelets to species when confidence in identification was high and otherwise as unidentified. Primary differences for 2010 were: we used 2 observers when possible and did not employ an independent observer; we reduced the maximum Beaufort sea state for sampling from 3 to 2; and we separately recorded flying groups (murrelets of 1 species class in a flock) only within a box extending 200 m to the front and sides of observers. We did not include flying groups in density or abundance estimates.

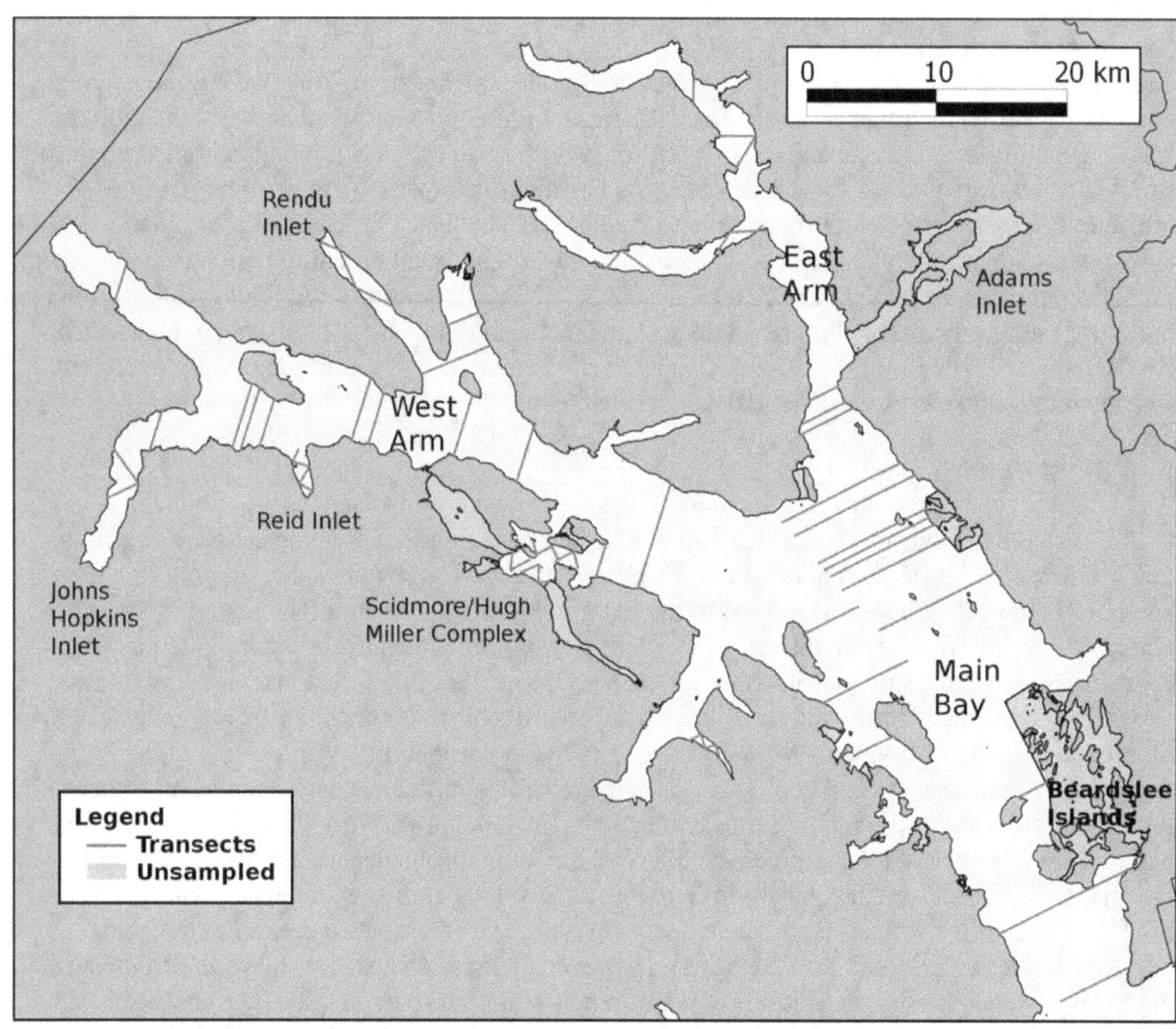

Figure 1. Sampling scheme for line transect surveys of murrelets within Glacier Bay, July 2010. Linear transects were used in open waters (>2.5 km wide) and zigzag transects were used in more restricted waters. Transects extended from shore to shore, except in the Main Bay, where some were split into 2 at mid-Bay to maintain optimal transect length. Linear transects were oriented perpendicular to the prevailing shoreline. The orientation of zigzag transects relative to shore was determined by width of each area.

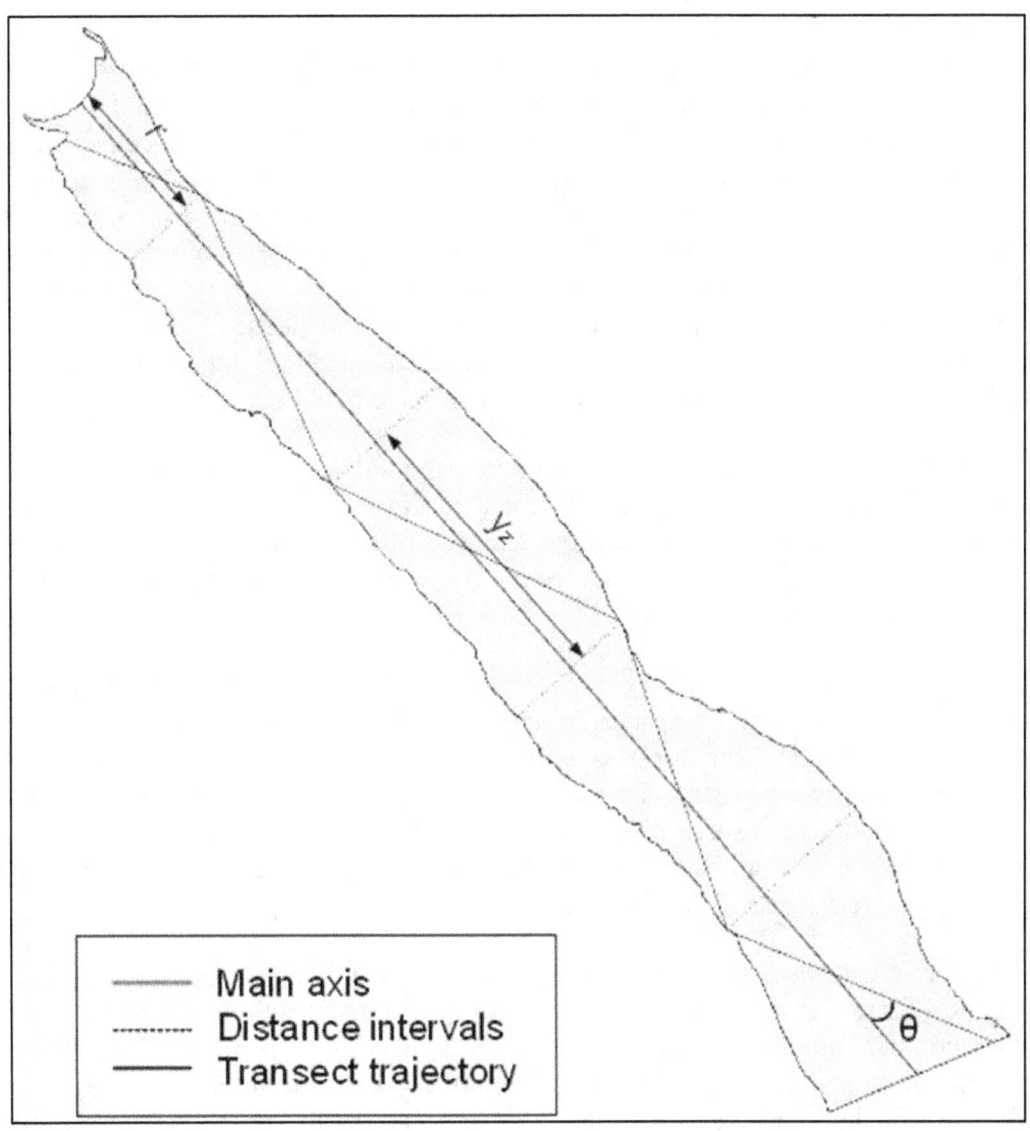

Figure 2. Layout of zigzag transect segments in Rendu Inlet. Transect segments met the shore at regular intervals y_z along the main axis of the fjord. Based on the width of each area, we adjusted y_z to provide suitable coverage probability and optimal angle of approach to shore $30° < \theta < 60°$. We combined segments to achieve desired transect length.

Analytic methods

We estimated detection probability and species-specific abundance using Program DISTANCE version 6.0 (Thomas et al. 2010) following methods outlined by Buckland et al. (2001). We modified these methods to account for incomplete detection near the transect center line ("center line") using methods similar to those described by Hoekman et al. (2011b). These adjustments assumed that species were correctly identified and that the proportion of each species in the identified and unidentified samples were the same. Because the latter assumption would be suspect if species differed in detection probability, we used AIC_c values (Burnham and Anderson 2002) to weigh support for 3 alternative models of detection functions: 1) species pooled (no difference in detection functions), 2) species separate (difference in shape and scale), and 3) species adjustment using scale covariate (difference in scale but not shape).

Density estimates were based on several component parameters: detection probability across the transect width, detection probability near the center line, average group size for each species class, and average encounter rates for each species class (assuming no covariance in encounter rates among classes). We estimated abundance for our study area by multiplying its area (1,170 km^2) by estimated densities.

We also took several steps to facilitate comparison of our data with previous studies in Glacier Bay. We generated strip transect estimates of density (Williams et al. 2002) using a 300 m strip width and the separate ratio estimator of Cochran (1977) to allow direct comparison to studies using these methods. For both line and strip transect density estimates, we projected abundance across an estimate of the total surface area of Glacier Bay (1,276 km^2) very similar to those used in previous studies (Drew et al. 2008, Kirchhoff 2008). This approach assumed areas surveyed by each study were representative of the entire Bay.

Finally, to explore how variation in probability of detection and identification may have contributed to variation among abundance estimates, we adjusted abundance estimates from prior studies that did not account for incomplete detection or identification. We used reported identification rates, but detection probability is unknown for strip transects. For these studies, we assumed reasonable but moderate detection probability in order to assess whether resulting negative bias could explain observed differences in abundance estimates relative to recent line transect surveys (see Appendix). To display the distribution of each species across surveyed transects, we plotted the location where each identified group was observed, with the diameter of each symbol proportional to group size.

Results

We surveyed 40 transects totaling 212.5 km between 8-16 July 2010 and detected 73 flying groups and 1,258 groups on the water. We classified 225 (18%) and 725 (58%) groups as Kittlitz's and marbled murrelets, and we classified 308 (24%) groups as unidentified. Poor visibility was common during surveys, with ~25% of observations recorded during mist or rain. Model selection results did not provide evidence supporting differences in detection functions between species, as models including differences explained little additional variation in these data and had much lower weight of evidence relative to a model pooling species (Table 1). For pooled murrelet groups, we truncated observations at 230 m from the center line, and detection probability was high within this distance (Table 2). Our estimated effective strip width was 144 m. Estimated detection probability remained near 1 to almost 100 m from the center line, but decayed rapidly at larger distances (Fig. 3).

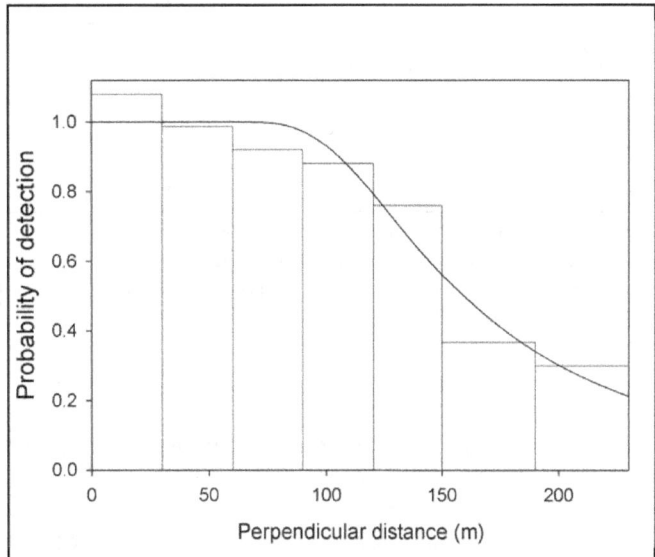

Figure 3. Estimated detection function for murrelets from line transect surveys in Glacier Bay, July 2010, showing probability of detection of murrelet groups relative to perpendicular distance from the center line.

Higher average group size and encounter rates for marbled murrelets (Table 2) resulted in estimates of density and abundance >400% higher than Kittlitz's murrelets (Table 3). Estimated precision was also slightly higher for marbled (CV = 0.087) than Kittlitz's murrelets (CV = 0.102). Changes to methods in 2010, particularly use of the local variance estimator, increased precision of estimates relative to 2009. Variation in encounter rate accounted for most of the total variance in density estimates, with variance in estimates of group size and detection across the transect width and near the center line making similar contributions to overall variance (Table 4).

Our estimates of abundance using strip transect methods were substantially lower than from line transects (Table 5) but were substantially higher than strip transect estimates from 1999-2007. Adjusted estimates for marbled murrelets from 2009-2010 on average were almost 150% higher than estimates from 1999-2007. Estimates for Kittlitz's murrelets from 2009-2010 were at or slightly above the range of variation from previous years and on average were ~75% higher than estimates from 1999-2007. Adjusted abundance estimates from 2009-2010 generally were similar between studies and years.

The distribution of Kittlitz's murrelets within Glacier Bay was extremely patchy (Fig. 4). The highest densities were encountered in the central portions of the mid and lower main bay and in the upper West Arm in and around Reid Inlet. Marbled murrelets were encountered throughout Glacier Bay, but densities were very high in the mid- to lower Main Bay (Fig. 5).

7

Table 1. Selection results for models examining detection functions for Kittlitz's versus marbled murrelets from line transect surveys in Glacier Bay, July 2010.

Model[a]	-2 log{likelihood}	ΔAIC$_c$[b]	AIC$_c$ weights[c]	K[d]
Pooled	3019.8	0.0	0.62	3
Separate	3018.0	2.2	0.21	5
Scale Covariate	3020.3	2.5	0.18	4

[a]Models denoted by treatment of species differences.
[b]Differences in AIC$_c$ relative model with lowest value.
[c]Weight of evidence as being the actual best approximating model.
[d]Number of estimated parameters.

Table 2. Estimates for component parameters used to estimate density and abundance of Kittlitz's and marbled murrelets in Glacier Bay, July 2010.

Parameter	Estimate	SE	Degrees of freedom
Detection across transect width	0.72	0.02	1,239
Detection near transect center line	0.94	0.03	66
Group size			
Kittlitz's murrelet	2.05	0.08	223
Marbled murrelet	2.50	0.07	723
Unidentified murrelet	3.45	0.26	292
Encounter rate[a]			
Kittlitz's murrelet	1.17	0.1	39
Marbled murrelet	4.71	0.41	39
Unidentified murrelet	1.66	0.14	39

[a]Groups encountered per km.

Table 3. Estimated density and abundance of Kittlitz's and marbled murrelets on the water in the Glacier Bay, July 2010. Line transect survey methods accounted for probability of detection and species identification.

Species	Density[a]	SE	Sampled area[b] Abundance	SE	Glacier Bay[c] Abundance	SE
Kittlitz's murrelet	11.4	1.16	13,308	1,357	14,503	1,479
Marbled murrelet	52.7	4.59	61,717	5,372	67,259	5,854

[a]Individuals/km^2.
[b]Abundance extrapolated over 1,170 km^2 of sampled waters.
[c]Abundance extrapolated over 1,276 km^2 of Glacier Bay.

Table 4. Percent contribution of each component parameter to the total estimated variance of density estimates of Kittlitz's and marbled murrelets in Glacier Bay, July 2010.

Species	Encounter rate[a]	Group size	Detection across transect[b]	Detection near transect[c]
Kittlitz's murrelet	72	12	7	9
Marbled murrelet	68	10	9	13

[a]Groups encountered per km.
[b]Probability of detection within the right truncation distance, estimated from the detection function.
[c]Probability of detection near the center line, estimated from the independent observer experiment (Hoekman et al 2011).

Table 5. Recent estimates of abundance of Kittlitz's and marbled murrelets during the breeding season in Glacier Bay, assuming a surface area of ~1,276 km^2. Estimates from strip transect surveys did not account for probability of detection or species identification. Adjusted estimates accounted for these factors using reported identification rates and reported or assumed detection probabilities.

Source[a]	Year	% Identified[b]	Strip transects[c] Kittlitz's	Marbled	Adjusted[d] Kittlitz's	Marbled
This study	2010	76	8,374	44,706	14,503	67,259
Kirchhoff and Lindell *In Preparation*	2010	88			13,818	86,612
Hoekman et al. 2010	2009	47	5,624	11,711	15,333	33,854
Kirchhoff et al. 2010	2009	96	6,507	39,167	11,884	71,530
Kirchhoff 2008 (a)	2007	97			4,421	32,208
Kirchhoff 2008 (b)	2007	97	3,692	23,029	6,650	41,481
Drew et al. 2008[e]	2003	75	3,836	12,761	8,946	29,760
Drew et al. 2008[e]	2002	73	1,678	9,263	4,016	22,172
Drew et al. 2008[e]	2001	66	3,638	11,341	9,631	30,024
Drew et al. 2008[e]	2000	39	2,770	8,300	12,274	36,777
Drew et al. 2008[e]	1999	65	3,291	12,712	8,803	34,004

[a]Source material for strip transect estimates.
[b]Percent of individuals or groups identified to species.
[c]Estimates of abundance from strip transect surveys, typically with a 300 m strip width.
[d]Estimates of abundance adjusted to account for probability of detection and identification using line transect methods (this study, Hoekman et al. 2011a, Kirchhoff 2008 (a), Kirchhoff and Lindell *In Preparation*) or using adjustments to strip transect estimates as described in appendix (all others).
[e]Estimates included flying murrelets within 300 m strip widths.

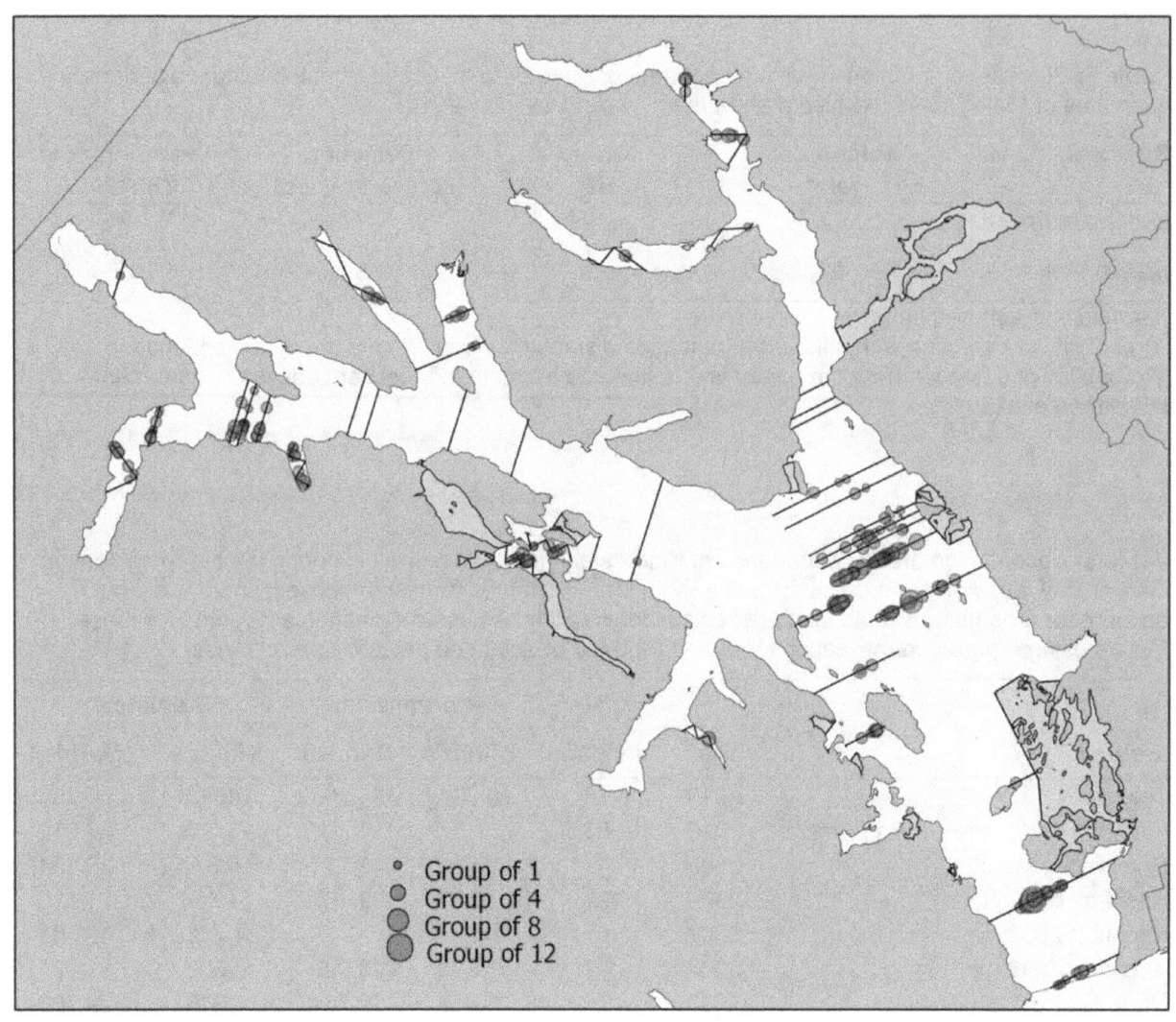

Figure 4. Distribution of Kittlitz's murrelets observed during line transect surveys in Glacier Bay, July 2010. The diameter of symbols is proportional to the size of the group. Areas shaded red were unsampled.

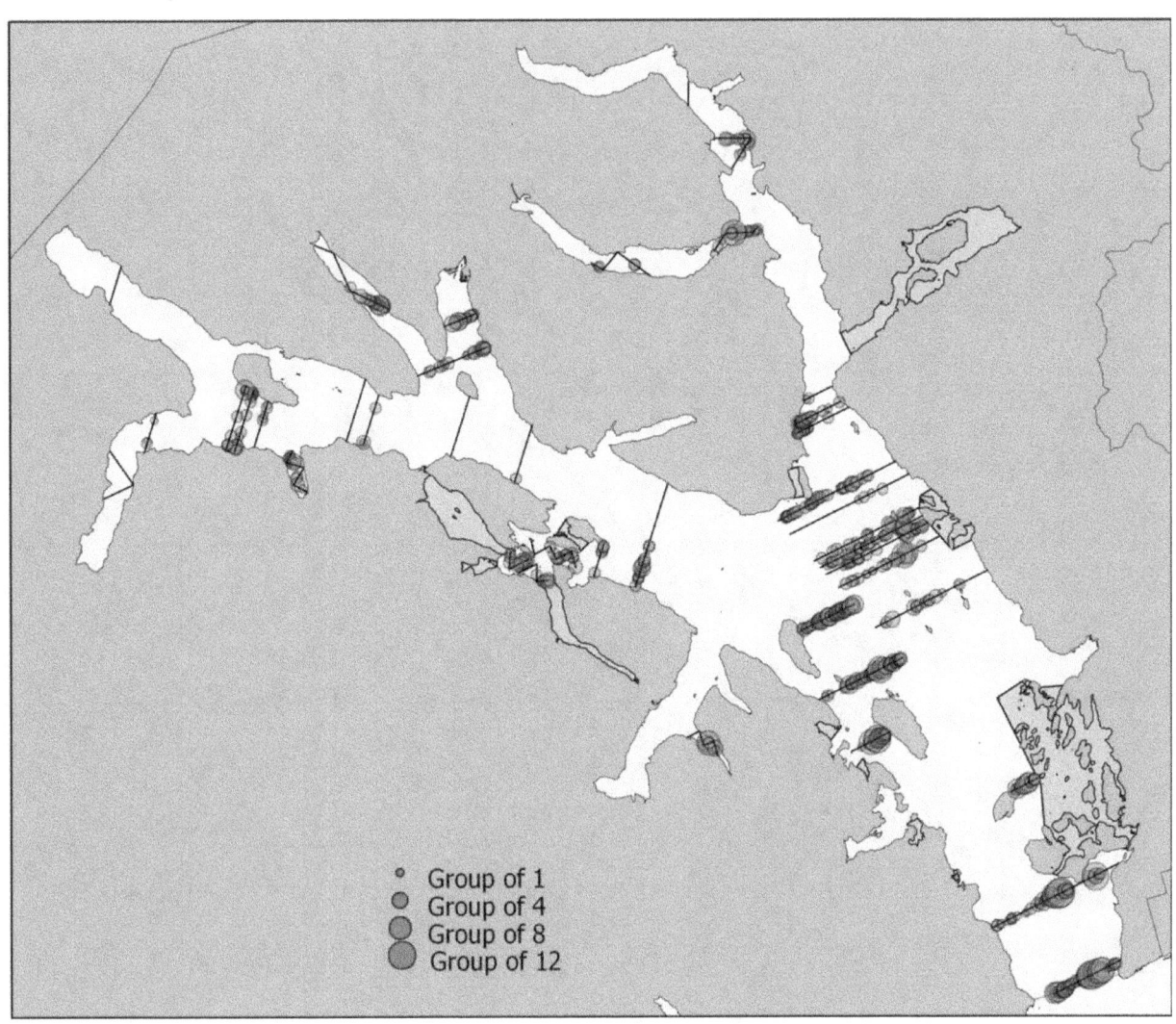

Figure 5. Distribution of marbled murrelets observed during line transect surveys in Glacier Bay, July 2010. The diameter of symbols is proportional to the size of the group. Areas shaded red were unsampled.

Discussion

The distribution and abundance of murrelets we observed in 2010 was atypical relative to recent historical data. Prior observations of highest concentrations of Kittlitz's murrelets in fjords of the upper Bay (Drew et al. 2008, Kirchhoff et al. 2010, Hoekman et al. 2011a) was consistent with their association with glacially-influenced habitats (Kuletz et al. 2003). In 2010, we found largest concentrations of both species throughout the main Bay, a pattern common for marbled murrelets but not previously observed for Kittlitz's murrelets (Drew et al. 2008, Kirchhoff et al. 2010, Hoekman et al. 2011a). These aggregations typically were far from shore or glacial outflow. Distributions of murrelets within Glacier Bay are characterized by ephemeral concentrations, likely where bathymetry and local conditions create high food availability (Zamon 2003, Arimitsu et al. 2007). We hypothesized murrelets responded to unusually productive foraging conditions in the main Bay.

Our 2010 abundance estimate for marbled murrelets in Glacier Bay was nearly double that from 2009 (Hoekman et al. 2011a). For a relatively k-selected species, this large increase was more plausibly explained by immigration to the local population than by high recruitment alone. Kirchhoff (2008) observed thousands of murrelets entering and exiting Glacier Bay daily, and murrelets in Alaska are known to travel over 100 km from nesting to foraging areas (Whitworth et al. 2000). Thus, large aggregations of marbled murrelets in the main Bay may have included many immigrants from outside Glacier Bay. Similar abundance of Kittlitz's murrelets between years suggested a shift in distribution.

Distributions of Kittlitz's murrelets in Glacier Bay have been patchy and variable among years, and spatial variation in encounter rates among transects has dominated variance of abundance estimates (Drew et al. 2008, Kirchhoff 2008, Kirchhoff et al. 2010, Hoekman et al. 2011a, this study). Despite similar sampling effort, precision of abundance estimates increased in 2010 relative to 2009 (Hoekman et al. 2011a), in large part because the local variance estimator minimized deleterious effects of spatial variation in encounter rates. As in 2009, dense concentrations of Kittlitz's murrelets occurred where expected densities were low. However, the local variance estimator coped with unpredictable spatial variation more effectively than geographic stratification (Hoekman et al. 2011a). Use of zigzag transects in 2010 also avoided short transects, which disproportionately contributed to variance in encounter rates in 2009. We found no clear relation between expected and observed encounter rates for Kittlitz's murrelets, indicating allocation of sampling effort had negligible influence on precision of estimates.

Comparison of recent abundance estimates for murrelets in Glacier Bay is complicated by differences in survey and analytic methods. Differences among in surveys in sampling design, survey timing, and methods of accounting for probability of detection, unidentified murrelets, and flying murrelets can have large effects on abundance estimates. Drew et al. (2008) and Kirchhoff et al. (2010) utilized non-probabilistic sampling designs, and thus their samples and results may not be representative of Glacier Bay, although use of a geographically-stratified estimator by Drew et al. (2008) reduced these concerns. Sampling frames have varied as well, meaning results apply to different areas within Glacier Bay. Romano et al. (2004) found evidence of increasing densities of marbled murrelets through the summer in parts of Glacier Bay, but densities of Kittlitz's murrelets appeared to peak in early July. Therefore, the mid-June surveys of Drew et al. (2008) may sample slightly smaller populations than surveys in July (Kirchhoff 2008, Kirchhoff et al. 2010, Hoekman et al. 2011a, Kirchhoff and Lindell *In Preparation*, this study). Strip transect methods employed by Drew et al. (2008) and Kirchhoff et al. (2010) did not account for incomplete detection or species identification. However, these have varied widely among studies, among years, across environmental conditions, and relative to number and ability of observers; failing to account for this variation results in large and variable negative bias in abundance estimates. Because flying birds move rapidly, studies including these in abundance estimates (Drew et al. 2008, Kirchhoff et al. 2010) introduced positive bias to estimates. Studies excluding flying birds (Kirchhoff 2008, Hoekman et al. 2011a, this study) suffered from negative bias, but flying murrelets likely accounted for only ~1-2% of populations (Kirchhoff 2008, Kirchhoff and Lindell *In Preparation*) indicating bias likely was small.

Estimates of murrelet abundance in Glacier Bay from strip transects have generally been higher for 2009-2010 relative to 1999-2003, indicating recent surveys have detected more identified murrelets within strips than older surveys. But, the extent to which increases reflected differences in rates of detection and species identification cannot be ascertained from strip transects. We feel it is more meaningful to compare our abundance estimates from line transects to strip transect estimates adjusted to account for incomplete detection and identification. However, these adjustments required several caveats. We used identification rates reported for each annual survey to adjust for unidentified murrelets, but we relied on plausible but untested assumptions (Hoekman et al. 2011a). Because detection rates were unknown, we assumed murrelet detection probabilities during multi-species strip transect surveys (Drew et al. 2008) matched a moderately low estimate from Kirchhoff (2008), and we assumed detection near the transect center line for all surveys matched our estimate from 2009 surveys (Hoekman et al. 2011a). Finally, we had no sampling variance estimates for most adjusted (historical) estimates, and we note most strip transect estimates have been relatively imprecise. Despite these caveats, we felt it prudent to adjust for differences in methods, even if imperfectly. We stress adjusted strip transect estimates served to give context to our 2009 and 2010 line transect estimates rather than to rigorously assess population status or trend. Assuming a moderately low detection probability for strip transects allowed us to place a plausible but high upper boundary on the extent to which strip transect may have under-estimated abundance.

Adjustments to historic abundance estimates resulted in substantial increases in all cases, with average increases of >100%. The magnitude of increases was inversely proportional to detection and identification rates. Adjusted estimates for both species were higher on average for 2009-2010 relative to 1999-2007. For marbled murrelets, large increases and little overlap in ranges suggested differences in survey methods alone could not plausibly explain differences in between periods and hence that populations likely have increased dramatically. For Kittlitz's murrelets, increases were smaller and ranges of estimates between these periods overlapped to a greater degree. Thus, the extent to which elevated estimates from 2009-2010 can be attributed to alternative explanations such as population increase, differences in methods, differences of timing of surveys, or imprecision of estimates remains uncertain. Despite markedly different sampling designs, separate surveys from 2009 (Kirchhoff et al. 2010, Hoekman et al. 2011a) and 2010 (Kirchhoff and Lindell In Preparation, this study) provided evidence of similarly high murrelet abundance. While effects of different methods on estimates cannot fully be resolved, our analyses strongly suggested that abundance estimates not accounting for probability of detection and identification likely suffered from substantial negative bias, that recent populations of marbled murrelets in Glacier Bay have increased, and that large increases in recent abundance estimates (relative to historical estimates) for Kittlitz's murrelets did not necessarily reflect increased population size.

Literature Cited

Agler, B. A., S. J. Kendall, and D. B. Irons. 1998. Abundance and distribution of marbled and Kittlitz's murrelets in south central and southeast Alaska. Condor 100:254-265.

Agness, A. M., J. F. Piatt, J. C. Ha, and G. R. VanBlaricom. 2008. Effects of vessel activity on the near-shore ecology of Kittlitz's Murrelets (*Brachyramphus brevirostris*) in Glacier Bay, Alaska. Auk 125:346-353.

Arimitsu, M. L., J. F. Piatt, M. D. Romano, and D. C. Douglas. 2007. Distribution of forage fishes in relation to the oceanography of Glacier Bay. Pages 102-106 *in* J. F. Piatt and S. M. Gende, editors. Proceedings of the Fourth Glacier Bay Science Symposium, October 26–28, 2004.

Buckland, S. T., D. R. Anderson, K. P. Burnham, J. L. Laake, D. L. Borchers, and L. Thomas. 2001. Introduction to Distance Sampling: Estimating Abundance of Biological Populations. Oxford University Press, New York, New York, USA.

Burnham, K. P., and D. R. Anderson. 2002. Model Selection and Multi-Model Inference, 2nd edition. Springer, New York, New York, USA.

Cochran, W. G. 1977. Sampling Techniques, 3rd edition. Wiley, New York, New York, USA.

Day, R. H., K. J. Kuletz, and D. A. Nigro. 1999. Kittlitz's Murrelet (*Brachyramphus brevirostris*), The Birds of North America Online (A. Poole, Ed.). Ithaca: Cornell Lab of Ornithology; Retrieved from the Birds of North America Online: http://bna.birds.cornell.edu/bna/species/435.

Drew, G. S., S. Speckman,, J. F. Piatt, J. M. Burgos, and J. Bodkin. 2008. Survey Design Considerations for Monitoring Marine Predator Populations in Glacier Bay, Alaska: Results and Post-hoc Analyses of Surveys Conducted in 1999-2003. Administrative Report. U. S. Department of the Interior, U. S. Geological Survey, Reston, Virginia, USA.

Hoekman, S. T., B. J. Moynahan, and M. S. Lindberg. *In Preparation*. Monitoring Protocol For Kittlitz's and Marbled Murrelets in Glacier Bay. Southeast Alaska Network, National Park Service, Juneau, AK.

Hoekman, S. T., B. J. Moynahan, M. S. Lindberg. 2011a. Monitoring Kittlitz's Murrelets in Glacier Bay National Park: 2009 Annual Report. Southeast Alaska Network, National Park Service, Juneau, Alaska, USA.

Hoekman, S. T., B. J. Moynahan, M. S. Lindberg, L. C. Sharman, and W. F. Johnson. 2011b. Line transect sampling for Murrelets: Accounting for incomplete detection and identification. Marine Ornithology 39:xxx-xxx.

Kirchhoff, M. D. *In Review*. On improving the power and accuracy of surveys for Kittlitz's murrelets *Brachyramphus brevirostris* in Alaska. Marine Ornithology 39:xx-xx.

Kirchhoff, M. 2008. Methodological considerations for at-sea monitoring of *Brachyramphus* murrelets in Glacier Bay, Alaska. Alaska Department of Fish and Game, Douglas, Alaska, USA.

Kirchhoff, M. D., and J. R. Lindell. *In Preparation*. Population abundance, trend, and important foraging habitat for Kittlitz's and Marbled Murrelets in Glacier Bay, Alaska, 1993-2010. Final Report to Glacier Bay National Park. Audubon Alaska, Anchorage, Alaska, USA.

Kirchhoff, M. D., M. Smith, and S. Wright. 2010. Abundance, population trend, and distribution of Marbled Murrelets and Kittlitz's Murrelets in Glacier Bay National Park. Audubon Alaska, Anchorage, Alaska, USA.

Kissling, M. L., M. Reid, P. M. Lukacs, S. M. Gende, and S. B. Lewis. 2007. Understanding abundance patterns of a declining seabird: Implications for monitoring. Ecological Applications 17:2164-2174.

Kuletz, K. J., S. W. Stephensen, D. B. Irons, E. A. Labunski, and K. M. Brenneman. 2003. Changes in distribution and abundance of Kittlitz's Murrelets *Brachyramphus brevirostris* relative to glacial recession in Prince William Sound, Alaska. Marine Ornithology 31:133-140.

Lindell, J. 2005. Results of at-sea *Brachyramphus* murrelet surveys in Icy Strait and other selected areas of Southeast Alaska. Final report. U. S. Fish and Wildlife Service, Ecological Services, Juneau, Alaska, USA.

Mack, D. E., M. G. Raphael, and J. L. Laake. 2002. Probability of detecting Marbled Murrelets at sea: Effects of single versus paired observers. Journal of Wildlife Management 66:865-873.

Moynahan, B. J., W. F. Johnson, D. W. Shirokauer, L. C. Sharman, G. Smith, and S. M. Gende. 2008. Vital Sign Monitoring Plan: Southeast Alaska Network. U. S. National Park Service, Fort Collins, Colorado, USA.

Piatt, J. F., K. J. Kuletz, A. E. Burger, S. A. Hatch, V. L. Friesen, T. P. Birt, M. L. Arimitsu, G. S. Drew, A. M. A. Harding, and K. S. Bixler. 2007. Status review of the Marbled Murrelet (*Brachyramphus marmoratus*) in Alaska and British Columbia. Open-File Report 2006-1387. U.S. Geological Survey, Reston, Virginia, USA.

Ronconi, R. A., and A. E. Burger. 2009. Estimating seabird densities from vessel transects: Distance sampling and implications for strip transects. Aquatic Biology 4:297-309.

Stevens, D. L., and A. R. Olsen. 2003. Variance estimation for spatially balanced samples of environmental resources. Environmetrics 14:593-610.

Stevens, D. L., and A. R. Olsen. 2004. Spatially balanced sampling of natural resources. Journal of the American Statistical Association 99:262-278.

Thomas, L., S. T. Buckland, E. A. Rexstad, J. L. Laake, S. Strindberg, S. L. Hedley, J. R. Bishop, T. A. Marques, and K. P. Burnham. 2010. Distance software: Design and analysis of distance sampling surveys for estimating population size. Journal of Applied Ecology 47:5-14.

U. S. Fish and Wildlife Service (USFWS). 2010. Species assessment and listing priority assignment form for Kittlitz's murrelets. Unpublished document. U. S. Fish and Wildlife Service, Anchorage, Alaska , USA.

Whitworth, D., S. Nelson, S. Newman, G. Van Vliet, and W. Smith. 2000. Foraging distances of radio-marked Marbled Murrelets from inland areas in southeast Alaska. Condor 102:452-456.

Williams, B. K., J. D. Nichols, and M. J. Conroy. 2002. Analysis and Management of Animal Populations, 1st edition. Academic Press, San Diego, California, USA.

Zamon, J. 2003. Mixed species aggregations feeding upon herring and sandlance schools in a nearshore archipelago depend on flooding tidal currents. Marine Ecology-Progress Series 261:243-255.

Appendix: Adjusting Strip Transect Estimates for Incomplete Detection and Species Identification

Many recent abundance estimates for Glacier Bay are from strip transects (Drew et al. 2008, Kirchhoff 2008, Kirchhoff et al. 2010). These methods do not account for probability of detection or species identification and likely introduce large negative bias to estimates (Hoekman et al. 2011b). Substantial variation in detection and identification rates among studies and among years within studies (Drew et al. 2008, Kirchhoff 2008, Hoekman et al. 2010, Kirchhoff et al. 2010, this study) has complicates comparison among abundance estimates and hence inference about population status and trend. To facilitate comparisons, we used simple methods to adjust estimates from strip transects for incomplete detection and identification. Based on reported identifications rates, we allotted unidentified murrelets to species-specific abundance estimates assuming identical proportions of each species in the identified and unidentified samples (similar to Hoekman et al. 2011b). Strip transect methods do not allow estimation of detection probability, but line transect surveys in Glacier Bay have shown wide variation in detection probability (Kirchhoff 2008, Hoekman et al. 2011a, this study), and others have demonstrated variation in detection probability relative to number and skill of observers and environmental conditions (Mack et al. 2002, Kissling et al. 2007, Ronconi and Burger 2009, Hoekman et al. 2011a). For line transect surveys in Glacier Bay, we estimated detection probability P_a over the 300 m strip width commonly used for strip transects as:

$$\widehat{P}_a = \frac{\int_0^{150} \hat{g}(x)dx}{150} \tag{1}$$

where $g(x)$ is the detection function relative to distance x from the transect. We estimated P_a as 0.91 in 2010 (this study), 0.80 in 2009 (Hoekman et al. 2011a), and 0.61 in 2007 (Kirchhoff 2008). We attributed high detection in 2009 and 2010 to frequent use of binoculars to locate murrelets; we believe others have used binoculars primarily for identification. In addition, surveys of Drew et al. (2008) recorded all wildlife species and likely devoted less effort to detection of murrelets. Thus, we hypothesized their detection rate was moderate, and we applied the 2007 estimate to all strip transects. Furthermore, estimated abundances from Drew et al. (2008) were substantially lower than from 2009 and 2010, and we felt positing moderate detection was useful to ascertain whether differences in probability of detection and species identification could plausibly explain differences in abundance estimates between these periods. Hoekman et al. (2011a) estimated detection probability near the center line P_c was 0.94, which violated the distance sampling assumption of complete detection. We adjusted all strip transect estimates using this estimate. For each species $s = 1$ to 2, we estimated an adjusted abundance $\hat{A}'_s$ as:

$$\hat{A}'_s = \frac{\frac{\hat{A}_s}{(A_K+A_M)} \cdot \frac{(\hat{A}_K+\hat{A}_M)}{P_{ID}}}{\hat{P}_a\hat{P}_c} \tag{2}$$

where A_s, A_K, and A_M are abundances for species s, Kittlitz's, and marbled murrelets from strip transects and P_{ID} is the proportion of individuals identified to species.

NPS 132/107036, March 2011

Natural Resource Program Center
1201 Oakridge Drive, Suite 150
Fort Collins, CO 80525

www.nature.nps.gov

www.ingramcontent.com/pod-product-compliance
Lightning Source LLC
Chambersburg PA
CBHW080934290526
45795CB00007BA/2744